Life Coaching Activities and Powerful Questions

A Practical Workbook for Life Coaches and all involved in Personal Development

Phyllis Reardon M.Ed
Life Coach

CoachPhyllis.com Inc
Copyright 2010   Newfoundland Labrador, Canada

Copyright 2010 by Phyllis E Reardon, CoachPhyllis.Com Inc.

All rights reserved. No part of this book may be reproduced, stored in a retrieval system or transmitted in any form of media, or electronic format without the prior written permission of Phyllis E. Reardon.

This is a personal development book and as such is not intended as a therapeutic tool.

Life Coaching Activities & Powerful Questions

A Practical Workbook for Life Coaches and all involved in Personal Development

ISBN: 1449909426
EAN-13: 9781449909420

Publishing Date: September, 2010

Life Coaching Activities & Powerful Questions

A Workbook

A Practical Workbook for Life Coaches and all involved in Personal Development

Acknowledgements

To my first Life Coaches, my parents, Dan and Hilda Reardon, who continually helped me see, my potential.

Thanks to Tom, Danny, Sean, Al, Marla and Rosemary.

Phyllis

Life Coaching Activities & Powerful Questions

This book takes you through the Life Coaching process in terms of definitions, quotes, activities, exercises and Coaching Questions as designed by CoachPhyllis.com Inc. Also included are Note sections so you can make your comments on what worked best for you.

I invite you to share these Life Coaching skills with friends and family. Please use this book to focus on your life and make it the best it can be.

"Life is change. Growth is optional. Choose wisely."

Karen Kaiser Clark

Table of Contents

Table of Contents

Introduction	2
What is Life Coaching?	5
Success	8
Success Activities	10
Success Questions	12
Visioning Your Future Self	13
The Wheel of Life	15
Coming Attractions Activities	16
Creating Your Vision Activity	18
Vision Questions	20
Strategic Planning	21
Strategic Planning Activity	24
Goal Setting Activity	26
Creating Accountability	29
Creating Accountability Activity	31
Completion Record	32
Structures and Rewards	33
Planning/Goal Questions	35
Self Belief	36
Increasing Self Esteem Activity	39
Self Concept/Self Esteem Questions	41
Positive Mental Attitude (PMA)	42
PMA Activity	45
PMA Questions	48
Persistence	49
Increasing Persistence Activity	52

Life Coaching Activities & Powerful Questions

Persistence Questions	53
Mind Set	54
Mind Set Activity	57
Mind Set Questions	59
Communication	60
Enhancing Communication Activity	63
Communication Questions	66
Multiple Intelligences (MI)	67
MI Activity	70
Careers and MI	72
Perception	73
Shifting Thinking Activity	75
Perception Questions	76
Work/Life Balance	77
Life /Work Balance Activities	78
Work/Life Balance Questions	79
Focus and Attention	80
Focus/Attention Activities	83
Affirmations	84
Affirmation Activity	86
Life Quotes	87
Goal Sheets	93
Wheel of Life Diagram	97
What's Next In Life?	98
Conclusion	102
Articles	103
The Author	110

Life Coaching Activities & Powerful Questions

Life Coaching Activities & Powerful Questions

"To be able to look back on one's life in satisfaction is to live twice."

Khalil Gibran

Introduction

Life Coaching has offered me an opportunity to see and explore the world with a different set of eyes.

"The real act of discovery lies, not in finding new lands, but in seeing with a new set of eyes." Marcel Proust

I have come to learn and understand the words of Socrates,

"The enlightenment is not in the answer but in the question."

Also I have discovered how powerful Questions can be in directing our life.

The process of Life Coaching that I use consists of a set of skills that if understood, practiced and used daily will enhance not only our lives but those whom we interact with at work and in life. These skills consist of:

Success Strategies
Visioning
Strategic Planning
Self Belief
Communication
Persistence
Perception
Mind Set
Work/Life Balance
Attending/Focus
Personal Strengths
Positive Mental Attitude

Life is not simple nor is it easy. We need knowledge and support along the way to achieve to our full potential. There are so many parts to life, both physical and emotional, that we cannot be expected, at an early age, to know and understand how each and everyone operates and how we can get the most from them.

Life is Learning. Life is Change. Life is Challenge.

Use this book in a way that best suits your needs. You can start at the beginning and work through, or you can pick topics of interest. Each part of the book can be a stand alone.

Although this book is designed specifically for Life Coaches, anyone involved with the personal development field can make extensive use of the Activities and Powerful Questions sections.

This book is designed as a resource for Life Coaches, Teachers, Guidance Counselors, School Counselors, Human Resource Personnel and Parents.

Your Life is Precious.

Get the Most from it.

What is Life Coaching?

"Tell me what you plan to do with your one wild and precious life?"

Mary Oliver

What is Life Coaching?

Life Coaching is a possibilities building relationship, between a life coach and a client, for the purpose of improving the client's life and work.
Life Coaching helps individuals create the changes they want in all aspects of their lives. It is a process that helps clients get unstuck and move plans forward to successful completion.

So we can say that:

Life Coaching is moving people toward *success*.
Life Coaching is a *focus* on the *future*.
Life Coaching is all about *change*.
Life Coaching moves people from *idea to action*.
Life Coaching is an *ongoing* relationship, between coach and client, which focuses the client on taking action toward the realization of their goals or *desired self*.
Life Coaching is a platform or vehicle for learning.

How Life Coaching Works

People hunger for positive change, but in their busy lives they find it difficult to take the necessary steps to make that change. Research has shown that the more clearly defined an individual's future, the more likely they are to achieve their goals. Clearly defined goals in work and life lead to more successful business and individuals. However, clearly defined goals of their own do not guarantee success; we have just to reflect on New Year resolutions. For the most part they fail not because goals were not clearly defined or individuals not successful people, they fail because the process or strategies people employed were unsound or unsuitable.

With a focus on the future individuals are supported through the Life Coaching process in the development of successful strategies for implementing and maintaining desired life and work changes.

The coaching process allows clients to stop everything they are doing and take a close look at their lives; evaluate what they want and check the direction in which they are headed.

Through a series of individual sessions, the life coaching process challenges, inspires and supports the client in achieving their goals, while at the same time holding them accountable.

Just by the very nature of human beings, we are more likely to complete tasks that are being monitored by another person. This is accountability, and it is built into the coaching process.

Clients are assisted in expanding the view of themselves by recognizing their own potential, and clearly defining action or actions that will transform their potential into success.

Life Coaching is not counseling nor is it therapy.

"Most people know what they want but they don't know how to achieve it."
Coach Phyllis

Success

"Success is desiring something and then accomplishing it."

Coach Phyllis

What is Success?

> *"Both success and failure are largely the results of habit."*
>
> Napoleon Hill

Success is different for everyone.

Success can be defined as achieving what you want to achieve; this can range from baking the perfect chocolate cake to creating a multimillion dollar business.

The Success depends on the stated Goal.

Success, however, is not possible without planning, nor is it possible without understanding our personal role in directing our life. Each and every one of your clients has the potential to achieve whatever it is they choose. Success and the feeling of success comes from fulfilled potential.

In relationship to human development, 'potential' means having a possibility, the capability or personal power to achieve that which is planned to be achieved. It is like the potential for electric/hydro power that exists in a great waterfall. It remains potential until structured through an engineering process. Each any every individual has tremendous power, I like to call the 'waterfall syndrome,' which will stay a potential until we can direct that power to a useable source in creating our personal success.

Success depends on coming to recognize their full potential; individual skills, abilities and personal power. It is in discovering and understanding their ability that the client gets the power to be successful.

Your client needs to understand that no one else can create their lives for them. No one else has that power! They have a life time to create their successes.

Activity Success

Fill in your thoughts and answers to the following questions. Remember there are no wrong answers. Also remember success come in all sizes.

1. When have you been successful?
_____
_____
_____
_____
_____
_____
_____

2. What was your success/what were your successes?
_____
_____
_____
_____
_____
_____
_____

3. What led to this success?
_____
_____
_____
_____
_____
_____

4. What did you have in place to make this success happen?
_____
_____
_____

5. What were you like when this success happened?

_____
_____
_____
_____
_____

6. Do you know people who are successful? What are their successes?

_____
_____
_____
_____
_____

Life Coaching Questions for Creating Success

1. What do you really, really, really want?

2. Why do you want it?

3. What is success to you?

4. What does it look like?

5. How will you know when you have become successful?

6. How will you know when you have found it?

7. What is holding you back from getting it?

8. Do you believe you can get it?

9. What motivates you?

10. What are your intelligences and talents?

11. How can you make the greatest difference in your own life?

12. Who do you have to *become* in order to achieve what you *want* to achieve?

13. What has to be modified within you?

14. What change in your thinking has to take place?

15. What change in your personality has to take place?

16. What new knowledge do you need to gain?

17. What new skills do you need to learn?

Visioning Your Future Self

"Trust yourself. You know more than you think you do."

Dr. Spock

Visioning Your Future Self

> *"Our aspirations are our possibilities."*
> *Robert Browning*

Planning is key to success in life and work and an essential part of planning, is knowing in which direction you are headed, Your Vision or Possible Self.

Everything that has ever been created began as an idea or an image in someone's mind. Without a Vision of where we want to go or what we want to do, we can become uncertain and spend more time thinking about our future than actually taking action to make it happen. Many people move through their life in "reaction mode" never giving a thought to what they really want in their own life. This may seem like the easy way to function but they give up their power to choose and to design their own life.

Common knowledge teaches us that we can't hit a target we cannot see, so if we don't know where we want to be in the future (our target) chances are we won't reach it.

In Lewis Carroll's book, *Alice In Wonderland*, Alice asks The Cat which way she should go.

Alice: Would you tell me, please, which way I ought to go from here?
The Cat: That depends a good deal on where you want to get to.
Alice: I don't much care where.
The Cat: Then it doesn't much matter which way you go.

Circumstances, many times dictate an unwanted life path, but we have the power to change direction.

Activity   Wheel of Life

Our life consists of many parts, neither can be seen or function separate from the other. Try as you may to make a distinction between work and life and you will find in time that one inevitably influences the other.

Life Coaching is a holistic process, how could it be any other way? In my practice, I have my clients complete the Wheel of Life. The Wheel I present consists of 8 parts. Use page 97 diagram.

In your life there may be more or there may be less parts. For this activity label each section of the Wheel from the list below. Then indicate using the scale from 1-10 where you feel you are in your life/work.
One (1) being low; 10 being high. Now connect the dots.

What shape is your Wheel? Would this Wheel give you a smooth ride in Life or a rough ride?

Life Parts

Family/Relationships
Career/Work
Health/Fitness
Personal Growth
Money/Finances
Physical Environment
Fun/Joy
Romance

Activity   Coming Attractions

"Your imagination is a preview of your life's coming attraction."
                                                          Albert Einstein

Creating your Future self....your vision

1. What do you really, really want?

_____
_____
_____
_____
_____
_____

2. What do you see your future self looking like?

_____
_____
_____
_____
_____
_____

3. What would you do if you knew you couldn't fail?

_____
_____
_____
_____

Life Coaching Activities & Powerful Questions

4. What is your passion?

_____
_____
_____
_____
_____
_____

5. When do you want this? 1 year, 5 years, 10 years?

_____
_____
_____

6. Which possible self do you want to avoid?

_____
_____
_____
_____
_____

7. What do you have to have in place to make all of this happen?

_____
_____
_____
_____

Activity   Creating Your Vision

What do you really, really want?   Reflect on all parts of your life and work. Revisit Your Wheel of Life.

Life_____
_____
_____
_____
_____
_____

Work_____
_____
_____
_____
_____
_____

Now complete the following activity.

A. *Visualize*: This is not always easy for some people, but try to get a picture in your head, your thoughts of what your life/career would look like.

What would you be doing?
Where would you be working?
Where would you be living?
What would you be wearing?
What would your life be like when you successfully complete this goal?

_____
_____
_____
_____
_____

B. *Pen It*: Write it down on paper.

Writing it on paper can make it more real to you, take it out of your head and put it on paper.

What does this life/ career look like?

Describe what you would be doing at this work, where you would be living.

What would your life be like when you successfully complete this goal?

Our energy flows where our attention goes. **Be sure to Post this description in your office, bedroom or someplace where you will see it as a constant reminder. Insure that what you want to achieve in life and work is in the forefront of you day in day out.**

C. *Tell a trusted friend*

You might want to tell a trusted friend about your vision, your idea, your plan, as this creates some accountability. Ask them to check on you to see how you are progressing.

D. *Memorize It*: *Make it yours!*

You have to really believe that you are going to reach this life/career goal so memorize what you have written. Get it in your subconscious. You are more likely to behave in the direction of the goal if you have the visual in your subconscious. Everyday tell yourself you are the best (name the title/career). Practice describing your new title/ career to a friend. Make it is yours!

Life Coaching Questions for Creating Your Vision

1. What do you want in life and work?

2. What will your life/work look like in the future?

3. What are your desired outcomes?

4. What will your life/work be like in 5 years? 10 years? 20 years?

5. What will your grandchildren say about you?

6. What are your possibilities for work?

7. Why do you want this lifestyle?

8. How will you benefit from this kind of work?

9. Do you need anyone to help you achieve this vision?

10. What will the people in your life think about your vision?

11. How will you feel about yourself when you achieve this lifestyle?

12. When do you want this vision to materialize?

13. What is your personal Mantra at this time?

14. What will be your personal mantra in 10 years?

Strategic Planning

"Things rarely get stuck because of lack of time. They get stuck because the doing of them has not been defined."

David Allen

Strategic Planning

"The ancestor of every action is a thought."

Ralph Waldo Emerson

Vision is necessary but not sufficient. Your Vision becomes your Goal.

There are some new age programs that may lead you to believe that if you create a 'wished for' vision and concentrate on that vision long enough, it will come to you. Sounds nice and easy, even too good to be true? And you know what they say, if it is too good to be true, than it is not true.

Success, and remember this is any degree of success, can only be achieved by planning. *Successful people make plans for success.* **True success comes from Vision, but it needs a Strategy.**

Sometimes *Vision* **can be seen as dreaming or drifting;** *Strategy* **is planning and action. It involves strategic thinking. You may not realize it but you do this daily.**

Planning
Planning helps clarify the steps needed to reach our future self, that Vision you have created of your future. When planning consists of goal setting, action steps and timelines, it goes beyond day- to- day planning to become Strategic Planning.

Goals **or goal setting may not be the words you use often, more than likely you will say or hear people say: my summer project, personal projects, personal strivings etc. At the beginning of a New Year we hear much about New Year resolutions. Many people set goals but not everyone completes those goals. In fact research shows about 80% of New Year resolutions fail. Why does this happen? People truly** desire to make that change. What is needed to complete the goals?

Strategic Planning

We usually associate Strategic planning with big business or government but it is necessary for individuals in successfully reaching their goals.

A plan is what you say you will do.

A strategy is the how: action steps, timelines, resources.

Goals and next steps need to be written down on paper or entered into a computer, to get them out of your mind. If they stay in your head they can become fuzzy, unclear and not real and dissipate over a short time.

Be sure to:
Revisit. Rewrite. Revisit. Rewrite.

"Let our advanced worrying become our advanced thinking and planning."

Sir Winston Churchill

Activity   Strategic Planning

"If you don't plan, how will you know where to go?"
Coach Phyllis

1. What does planning mean to you?

_____
_____
_____
_____
_____
_____

2. How do you plan?

_____
_____
_____
_____
_____
_____

3. How should you plan?

_____
_____
_____
_____
_____
_____

4. Why should you plan?

_____
_____
_____
_____
_____
_____

5. What examples of planning do you use daily? Note below.

_____
_____
_____
_____
_____
_____
_____
_____
_____
_____
_____
_____
_____

Think

Dinner menu
Housework
Home repairs
To Do Lists
Exercise
Relaxation
Birthdays
Weddings
Conferences

Successful people make plans for Success!

Goal Setting

Revisit your *Vision* and your *Wheel of Life*.

Goals need to be written down on paper or entered into a computer to get them out of your mind. If they stay in your head they can become fuzzy, unclear and feel unrealistic.

 Writing Your Goals

What did you say you really, really want in life and work?

Goal Setting Activity

Write out your goals

*Goal
One*_____

*Goal
Two*_____

*Goal
Three*_____

*Goal
Four*_____

*Goal
Five*_____

Action Steps

For each goal, decide on the steps to be taken to reach these goals. List them.

Goal One Action Steps

Action Step One

_____
_____
_____

Action Step Two

_____
_____
_____

Action Step Three

_____
_____
_____

Action Step Four

_____
_____
_____

Action Step Five

_____
_____
_____

Life Coaching Activities & Powerful Questions

Now Prioritize the Action Steps. 1-5

_____
_____
_____
_____
_____

What is the NEXT STEP, the very next step?

_____
_____
_____
_____
_____

When defining steps break them down into the smallest pieces or actions. Take a defined action and then see if you can make smaller actions out of this one action step. This will help in successful completion.

This activity is to be completed for each of your stated goals.

Go to page 93.

Creating Accountability

"Talk does not cook rice."
Chinese Proverb

Creating Accountability

Timelines and Completion Dates

Accountability is key to success and therefore is an important part of the life coaching process, with each client learning to develop self- monitoring skills. It creates a structure to keep the client focused and moving forward, toward success.

In the Life Coaching process it is important to note that "accountability" is used for measuring a client's actions and in helping determine the degree of learning. The client self reports on their actions completed and skills, awareness and knowledge acquired. Accountability is not used in any way to judge the client. All is positive! All is for productivity!

Life coaching uses different techniques to keep the client accountable. Part of a well defined strategic plan is having timelines and completion dates in place. These are always defined by the client and must be realistic and appropriate to the needs of each individual client. There are no cookie cutters in Life Coaching. It should be noted that this process is used with both quantitative and qualitative goals.

Setting Timelines and Completion Dates

Timelines and Completion Dates are set for each of the *Action Steps*.

When setting timelines and completion dates it is essential that the client look at his or her past performance to discover what works best for them. Past performance can help predict the degree of completion times.

Activity Creating Accountability

Have the client think of a time when they completed a task.
What was in place to make this happen?
What was their life like at that time?
What steps did they take to insure completion?
Can they use the same process now with upcoming tasks?
What did they learn from past task completion?

Have clients determine their modus operandi (MO), their method of operating?
Do they procrastinate?
Do they make excuses?
How good are they at estimating time?
Do they complain about circumstances?

We usually tend to underestimate the amount of time it will take to complete tasks or actions and this can lead to lessened motivation. Encourage your client to be realistic.
Help them to determine what would work best for them.
Have them consider the time line and completion dates in the context of their everyday life.

When the defined action Is completed, make sure the client uses a *Check* mark to indicate the achievement and success. This action motivates and as the old adage goes, "nothing succeeds like success".

Activity Completion Record

Completion Record

Action(s) to Complete	Starting date	Completion date
1.		
2.		
3.		
4.		
5.		
6.		
7.		
8.		
9.		
10.		
11.		
12		
13.		
14.		
15.		

Structures and Rewards

"Celebrate any progress. Don't wait to get perfect."

                                    Ann McGee Cooper

Structures

Structures help us remember things. You know the classic structure- "tie a string on your finger". This may work for some. What can you use to help you remember actions to be completed?

Some examples may be: highly visible sticky notes, wearing your watch on the opposite arm, or rearranging and item in your office. Talisman, such as toys/figurines can be used as reminders of goals we need to reach.

What structures will work for you?

_____
_____
_____
_____
_____

They must be highly visible to be effective!

Rewards   The Law of Effect

Reward yourself. You deserve it! Rewards are based on the Law of Effect. The Law which states, you complete an action, you reward yourself, you feel good with the reward and guess what…you will want more rewards so you complete more actions. Learn to self reinforce- it will lead to success.

Take time to think about what might be a favorite reward of yours. It doesn't have to be exotic or extravagant; your favorite chocolate bar, a new CD, or an afternoon without the kids. If you wish, make note below.

_____
_____

Coaching Questions for Strategic Planning: Goal Setting-Action Steps-Accountability-Structures and Rewards

1. Are you getting the most value from your life?

2. Do you plan?

3. Do you have a Life Plan?

4. Do you have a daily plan?

5. Do you have a weekly plan?

6. What is your 5 year strategy for your life?

7. What kind of plan do you need to create?

8. What help or resources do you need?

9. What is your next step?

10. What is the best way for you to make this happen?

11. What should you try this time that you haven't tried before?

12. What does planning mean to you?

13. Why should you plan?

14. What examples of planning do you use every day?

15. What is your next step?

16. What structures would help you remember your to-do actions?

Self Belief

"If you can think it, you can achieve it."

Napoleon Hill

Self Belief

"If you think you can or can't, you're right."
                                        Henry Ford

Successful people believe they can achieve what they set out to do.

Successful people are very aware of themselves.

Self awareness is essential for success in our lives. We need to know ourselves from the inside out. We must develop a clear picture and understanding of our Self Concept and Self Esteem.

What is a belief?

A belief is the way you think all the time. Your beliefs started developing when you were very young and continue to this day. It is these beliefs that determine how you respond in everyday situations with family, friends, at work and in the world. Your beliefs are the source of your perceived limits and problems, but they are also the sources of joy and success.

Your *Self Concept* is what you believe yourself to be, your strengths, weaknesses, intelligences. Your Self Beliefs started forming shortly after birth with the love and interaction you received or did not receive from parent or guardian. As you entered school, the biggest social system you encountered at that time, your Self Belief became further influenced. Depending on how you were perceived by the school system, you either strengthened your Self Belief or it weakened.

All the comments from family, friends, teachers, schoolmates; all of your activities and experiences contributed either positively or negatively to your Self Concept, and created a foundation for later in life.

So right now, *who you believe you are is who you are.*

All of your interactions and beliefs about your self have created your *Self Esteem,* the value you place on yourself or how you view yourself at this present time.

This view may be totally positive, or it may be positive with some doubt; it may be partly negative or may be totally negative.

Your Self Esteem or Self Love will influence or effect your functioning in work and family, and will impact your success in life. The more positive your Self Esteem the better chance you have of having a happy successful life.

Remember, this success is always defined by you.

You have the power to increase and grow your Self Esteem/Self Concept.

"No one can make you feel inferior without your consent."
Eleanor Roosevelt

Activity — Ideas for Increasing Your Self Esteem

A. *Change negative self thoughts* to positive self thoughts. Stop the self criticism. Life is hard enough, be kind to yourself. Become aware of just how often you make negative comments about yourself that lessen your self esteem. At the end of each day make a Note of the negative comments you made about yourself and make a promise to eliminate these from your thoughts. You know the ones, 'why am I so stupid?' 'I just knew I'd get that wrong.' 'this is such an ugly dress, shirt', 'I'm so fat', you get the picture. Get rid of these self hurtful thoughts.

B. *Change your language* and you will change how you feel about you!
Try this activity.
Replace the word 'try' with 'I will do that';
Replace 'I can't' with 'I can';
Replace 'I should' with 'I will do that'

C. *Get Fit!*
Start an exercise program. Start small but start. The better you look the better you feel about yourself. Check with your doctor or health care provider.

D. *An Act of Kindness.*
Try this. You'll feel good and so will others and it's contagious.
Surprise your secretary, co-worker or friend with a morning coffee, muffin or homemade treat.
Treat your kids to a surprise dessert.
Leave a note of kind words on a loved one's pillow.
Mail an invite for a lunch/dinner date to friend/partner/spouse.
Smile at a senior on the street or grocery store.
Email/phone/write a note to a friend or family member you haven't seen for awhile.

E. *Take Action*
Anxiety and fear can keep you from moving forward and cause you to be unsatisfied with yourself. Try this. Next time you have a task to complete, no matter how small, create an action plan. Write down the answers to What, When, How. Now do it! Successfully completing tasks is a great self esteem builder. You feel good when you complete actions, no matter how small.

F. *Personal Affirmations*
Practiced daily personal affirmation can increase Self Esteem. Check page 84.

"The best place to succeed is where you are with what you have."

Charles Schwab

Coaching Question Self Esteem/ /Self Concept/Self Belief

1. How do you see yourself?

2. What are your strengths?

3. What can you do better than anyone else?

4. What makes you unique?

6. What are your weaknesses?

7. What do you believe about yourself?

8. What makes you different from other people?

9. What makes you the same?

10. What keeps you from winning?

11. If you were on a sports team, what contribution would you make?

12. What are you settling for in your life?

13. What are you denying about yourself or your life?

14. What is keeping you stuck?

15. When do you take your foot off the gas?

16. What do you expect of you?

17. What do you demand of you?

18. What can keep you moving forward?

Positive Mental Attitude

"It takes as much personal energy to be negative as it does to be positive. Choose to be Positive."
                                                                                                                        Unknown

Positive Mental Attitude

" A positive mental attitude (PMA) is the single most important principle of the science of success."
                                                            Napoleon Hill

An attitude or your attitude is how you place yourself in relation to other people and events around you. Let's face it, if you lived as a hermit you wouldn't even have to think about your attitude. Having a positive attitude helps you respond to people and events in a positive way. When you think and feel positively, you are more likely to create positive outcomes, therefore a positive mental attitude is key to your success.

Creating and maintaining a Positive Self is something like building and maintaining muscle, we have to practice it often. Did you know that if you stop working out you start to lose muscle in 72 hours? I think the same is true for a strong Positive Self - you must stay with it to keep a strong PMA.

Negative attitudes come at us from external and internal sources, so we must be prepared to rid ourselves of these negativities. You know the thoughts from within your own head or comments from others.

"Don't be silly, you can't do that."
"Who do you think you are?"
"You'll never be successful."
"You don't deserve it."

These thoughts may be present for various reasons, but you must learn to dissolve them or push then away. For many these thoughts arrive just before going to sleep. They are like nasty mosquitoes buzzing around in your head. You need to

learn how to get them out, destroy them and replace them with positive thoughts.
Think of it as a something like a dental floss but instead, it is a mental floss.

An important aspect and maybe the first step of creating a Positive Mental Attitude, is, believing you can. You, and only you have the ability to change how you think about yourself. But you must be open to this new you. And like the old adage, like a parachute, the mind works best when it is open.

Focus on your wins!

Your Positive Mental Attitude is probably the single most important thing to your success.

"They conquer, who think they can"
Ralph Emerson

Activity — Creating a Positive Mental Attitude

1. Think and write positive affirmations about yourself.

At the end of each day, reflect on your tasks and activities and note them in the form of positive statements. Such as:

'I'm an excellent interviewer/recruiter/sales person'.
'I am a great presenter/musician/teacher/.'
'I'm a wonderful mother/father/husband/wife/daughter.'
'I'm the best (name your occupation) in this city!'

_____
_____
_____
_____
_____
_____
_____
_____

2. Make a daily habit of saying or doing something to make someone else feel better or important. Think of people in your home, workplace, gym or shopping centre. Make a note of your positive comments.

_____
_____
_____
_____
_____
_____
_____
_____

3. Remember you always have a choice of how you respond in any and all situations; choose to respond in a positive way. Role play possible negative situations in which you respond in a positive way.

    a. *An irate driver cuts you off in traffic.*

Write a Positive Response

_____
_____
_____
_____
_____

    b. You are running late and someone skips you in line at the grocery store.

_____
_____
_____
_____
_____

4. Remember you can never control or change others, you can only control and change yourself. Think of times in relationships at home or work in which this was true for you. Note them if you wish.

_____
_____
_____
_____
_____

5. Keep your body fit and your mind will follow. Remember if you don't take time for fitness you will have to make time for illness! When you look good you feel good, when you feel good you develop a PMA.

6. Believe in your own ability. Develop and maintain a "Yes I can attitude." At the end of each day make a list of any negative thoughts you have had and next to each one write a positive thought. Make a habit of replacing negatives with positives.

Negative thought_____

Becomes Positive Thought_____

7. Learn from your mistakes without punishing yourself. There are no mistakes, only lessons. We learn from our experiences. What lessons have you learned over the past year? Note them on paper if you wish, if not make a mental list. Practice self - forgiveness and self - acceptance. No one else in the world is like you so why try to be like someone else!

_____
_____
_____
_____
_____
_____

Coaching Questions Positive Mental Attitude

1. What do you say to yourself, about yourself?

2. Is your self - talk positive or negative?

3. What is an example of your negative talk?

4. How can you replace this with positive thoughts?

5. When is the best time of day to reflect on your self - talk?

6. Do you use positive language while speaking to others?

7. Is the glass half full or half empty?

8. Do you see a cloudy day with some sun or a sunny day with clouds?

9. What do you choose to be today, positive or negative?

10. How do you choose to be with co-workers, positive or negative?

11. How do you feel around negative people?

12. How do you feel around positive people?

13. Do you sense any physical changes around negative people? What are they?

14. Do you sense any physical changes around positive people? Name them.

Persistence

"I am still learning".
Michelangelo

Persistence

"We can do anything we want to do if we stick with it long enough"

Helen Keller

The next step in becoming successful is Persistence or stick-to-itiveness.

Successful people never give up and if one way doesn't work they try another. This is the least sexy step to success, but just as essential as the others.

What thoughts come to mind when we hear the word 'persistence'?

What does it mean to you; hard work, keeping on keeping on, never giving up, giving 120%?

Sam Walton once said, about his Wal-Mart empire, *"it was an overnight success that was 20 years in the making."*

Michelangelo was quoted as saying, in reference to his masterpiece, David, *"if people only knew how hard I worked they wouldn't be so amazed."*

Whatever way we think of the word *Persistence,* it comes down to hard work at any level. Thomas Edison who developed 1093 patents before his success at inventing the light bulb said that, 'success is 1% inspiration and 99% perspiration.'

A very important aspect of persistence is *Commitment.*

Your success is very dependent on just how committed you are, without commitment you are only using half of your power to reach your goal, to achieve your success.

The greater your commitment, the great your degree of motivation;

the greater your motivation, the greater your staying power, or Persistence.

To help with maintaining Persistence, it will be necessary to review your Strategic Plan.

Check on stated actions.
Note your completions or successes.

One little action or success can lead to more success. You know the old adage, 'nothing succeeds like success.' But remember, there will be slips and bumps along the way.

I like this quote I read by unknown author, *'the road to success is dotted with many tempting parking spaces.'* There will be times when you will slip into one of these spaces. Take a break, but pull out and continue along the road to your success.

" Our greatest glory is not in never failing, but in rising every time we fall."

Confucius

Activity Tips to Increase Persistence

1. Think positively and be kind to yourself.

2. Review your goals weekly and note successes.

3. Surround yourself with positive people.

4. Avoid the naysayers in your life, they will pull you down.

5. Redo or update your physical environment. Even small changes help.

6. Post pictures or a list of what you want to achieve in life and work.

7. Persist.

8. Reward yourself.

9. Keep going.

10. Persist.

Coaching Questions Persistence

1. What motivates you?

2. What keeps you going?

3. How do you choose to work on your actions this day, week?

4. What is it to be passionate?

5. What is it for you to be persistent?

6. What is it to be focused?

7. What have you been withholding from yourself at work?

8. When are you dishonest with yourself?

9. What action are you avoiding?

10. What moved you ahead in the past?

11. What did success look like in past projects?

12. How committed are you to this action? Give a percentage.

13. Do you really want this outcome?

14. Do you need this outcome?

15. What are you doing to achieve it?

Mind Set

"Change your thinking and you'll change your world."
Norman Peale

Mind Set

> *"If you can think it, you can achieve it"*

What is your Operating System?

All of our computers function within an operating system, be it Windows 7, Windows XP, Windows Vista, Mac OS X etc. Within humans our Mind Set becomes the operating system. Our Mind Set consists of our beliefs, attitudes and assumptions about the world that have developed from all of our life experiences. Mind Set can be seen as a pair of eye glasses that create our view of the world. Mind Set influences how we react and respond to others and events in our life.

Our Mind Set consists of our beliefs (positive or negative), our Self esteem (our view of self) our level of persistence, and our attitude. All of these form our operating system.

As life coaches we need to understand our own operating systems or mind set before we can coach. You need to know just how you operate or respond in differing situations. You need to know how you feel in different situations. You need to know just how you see the world.

Is your operating system one of a deficit or an abundance model?

Mind Set is your habitual way of thinking, feeling and responding.

I firmly believe we all have tremendous potential, but unfortunately some of us don't get to reach our full potential. To succeed we may need to change our operating system, we may need to change the way we think. This is not easy, as our thoughts about self have been developing from the day we were born, and for some of us that is quite a few years. Not an easy task, but doable and necessary if we are to achieve what we said we really, really want in life.

What you think influences what you believe;

What you believe influences or determines your actions.

Therefore, how you think is crucial to your success.

"The more I want to get something done, the less I call it work."

Richard Bach

Life Coaching Activities & Powerful Questions

Activity Determining and Changing Mind Set

1. Have your client make a list (written or verbal) of their beliefs about their body.

_____
_____
_____
_____

2. Have your client give you a report or how they feel about their personal health.

_____
_____
_____
_____

3. Have the client make a list (written or verbal) of what they do to practice self care.

_____
_____
_____
_____

4. Ask a controversial question related to life/work/relationships.

How would you feel if....?

What would you think about……?

How would you react if…?

Where are these beliefs coming from?

5. Using this same controversial topic ask:

What are your assumptions around this issue?

What are other possible ways of thinking about this issue?

What are other ways of reacting?

6. Work Place Scenario

You get an email, late afternoon '*your manager wants to meet with you in the morning.*'

1. List your thoughts.

2. Create a positive list of possibilities with positive responses.

3. Note the worst possible thing that could happen and write a measured response.

7. Have clients practice "self talk"... Yes I can.

8. Change your language and you change your thinking with the use of daily Affirmations and Actions.

Mindset Coaching Questions

1. Is your glass half full or half empty?

2. Is it a great day or an okay day?

3. Are you full of hope or fear?

4. Do you believe in yourself or are you filled with self-doubt?

5. What is your operating system?

6. Does it need to be modified or upgraded?

7. Is your operating system user friendly?

8. Are all of your actions fear based?

9. Where is your attention?

10. Are you withholding yourself from life?

11. What is hard work for you?

12. What is persistence?

13. What else can you do to lead to success?

14. What are you missing in your work?

15. What have you learned about yourself?

Communication

"The single biggest problem with communication is the illusion that it has taken place."

George Bernard Shaw

Communication

"Most conversations are just alternate monologues. The question is, is there any real listening going on."
Leo Buscaglia

The technology age has brought a whole new meaning to the concept of communication. We can phone, email, text, IM, Skype….. Technology has made the world a smaller place and has increased the level of and changed the form of communication forever. No matter what the form, the basic skills of communication need to be acquired and enhanced.

Be it verbal or written, communication is the basis of all relationships at home, at work and in all aspects of our life.

As Simon and Garfunkel sang, '*No man is an Island*,' and as such, we are interacting with other humans from the time we are born. We go from a non-verbal to verbal communication at an early age and then by choice we can alternate from one form to another.

To be successful in work and life, we need to develop Effective Communication. Essential to effective communication is listening.

We need not only to 'listen to' but we also need to 'listen with' the person/client.

As Leo Buscaglia said, "most conversations are just alternate monologues".

People tend to half listen and then go on pause until it is there turn to speak. Most of us can't wait until the other person is finished so we can add our piece of information or two cents worth. The common phrase we have all heard, "you think that's bad, that's nothing compared to what happened to me." Each and every one of us has developed our own way of communicating. We will have phrases, intonations, and gestures that have been learned within our family or social settings. These may or not be effective and they indeed may not even be socially acceptable.

To be effective and succeed in life and work we must become aware of:

Our spoken/written language
How we articulate
Our body language
How we listen

"The greatest motivational act one person can do or another is listen."

Roy Moddy

Activities   Enhancing Communication

1. Become aware of how you speak. Self awareness is essential to change. Listen to yourself speak at work and at home and note the words and phrases you use.

_____
_____
_____
_____
_____
_____

Do this for a week. Do you need to change anything? Delete or add where needed.

_____
_____
_____
_____
_____
_____

2. Listen to the work/business words used by co-workers. Listen to work/business words used by your manager. Incorporate into your vocabulary. Talk the talk.

_____
_____
_____
_____
_____
_____

3. Add 5 new words a week to your vocabulary. If you have kids this can become a family game. Introduce one word a night, post it, discuss the meaning and how it should be used. Use it in a sentence. Make it yours.

a._____
b._____
c._____
d._____
e._____

4. Keep a dictionary or use a web dictionary to check new words that you hear. Create your own list of words - your own dictionary.

_____
_____
_____
_____
_____
_____

5. If you have to meet with someone, rehearse in front of a mirror what you plan to say. Note your expression and tone.

6. Practice listening skills. Listen to and with the speaker, determine what is being said that you can't hear in their words. Listen between the lines.

7. Practice facing the speaker directly. Keep eye contact, if culture permits.

8. Try not to interrupt. It is so tempting, but be patient.

9. Make mental notes of what the speaker is saying. Ask questions if you need to get clarification.

10. Use "I" language. Using "I" language is always a very safe way to explore a situation with another person.

11. Listen to documentaries, read news items. Make notes. Keep informed. Use this information during coffee breaks to begin a discussion.

12. Read as much as times permits. Use the words you read. Make sure you use them in the correct context.

13. Check out online dictionaries. They hold a wealth of information. Put them to work for you.

Coaching Question Enhancing Communications

1. How well do you communicate your ideas to others?

2. Do you enjoy speaking?

3. What areas are you comfortable talking about?

4. How do you feel when you are talking about a favorite subject?

5. What gives you this level of comfort?

6. Would this work when you speak about unfamiliar topics?

7. What would you need in place to make that happen?

8. Do you talk to yourself?

9. Do you need to increase your vocabulary?

10. What's your preferred style of communication; verbal, non-verbal?

11. Do you truly listen to what the other person is saying?

12. Do you use "I" language?

13. Are you a monologue waiting to happen?

Multiple Intelligence

"You are smarter than you think."

Coach Phyllis

Multiple Intelligence and Life Coaching

Understanding Your Multiple Intelligences

Much of the research around career and work states that if we are employed in work that is closely related to what we love to do, or to one of our strengths, we are more like to be highly successful at that work or career.

We are smarter than we think and have many more strengths than we give ourselves credit. Dr. Howard Gardner in 1983 defined eight multiple intelligences which are listed below.

According to the Multiple Intelligence theory, we have all eight intelligences, some of which are stronger than the others.

Many times our clients can struggle with determining their strengths. I have found that helping clients develop an understanding of their Multiple intelligences (MI) can increase their view of their own potential in relation to their career.

The Eight Intelligences as Defined by Howard Gardner and related occupations.

Musical: the ability to perceive, discriminate, transform and express musical forms.

Naturalist: the ability to understand, relate to, categorize, classify, and explain the things encountered in the world of nature.

Verbal/Linguistic: the ability to use words effectively either orally or in writing.

Logical/Mathematical: the ability to use numbers effectively and to reason well.

Interpersonal: the ability to perceive and make distinctions in the moods, intentions, motivations and feelings of other people.

Intrapersonal: the ability to form accurate self-understanding and to use this knowledge for effective functioning in life.

Visual/Spatial: the ability to perceive the world accurately and to create internal mental pictures.

Bodily/Kinesthetic : the ability to learn by doing, the ability to handle *objects* skillfully and use the body to express emotion as in dance, body language and sports.

Activity: Multiple Intelligences

Now that you have read the eight intelligences, reread and decide which three describe you. Note them on paper. Use the following list of related occupations to find an area of interest.

The Eight Intelligences and some related occupations or career areas.

Verbal/Linguistic:
Linguist, writer, radio or TV announcer, politician, poet, historian, folklorist, literary critic, philosopher, humanist, author, editor, speaker, playwright, attorney, journalist, talk-show host, storyteller, translator, reporter, lecturer, teacher, executive leadership, interpreter, librarian.

Logical/Mathematical:
Scientist, engineer, mathematician, physicist, tax accountant, researcher, statistician, astronomer, computer programmer, computer analyst, logician, math/science teacher, detective, economist, medical doctor, technologist, cataloguer.

Interpersonal:
Police officer, helping professions, politician, executive, teacher, therapist, travel agent, counselor, psychologist, novelist, psychiatrist, salesperson, social worker, business person, actor, community organizer, arbitrator. public relations, administrator, nurse, sociologist.

Intrapersonal:
Introspective novelist, psychologist, police officer, self-employment, executive, researcher, leadership, theorist, entrepreneur, philosopher, theologian, therapist.

Visual/Spatial:
Sailor, mathematical topologist, engineer, physical scientist, surgeon, chess player, sculptor, commander, cartographer, theoretical physicist, architect, art historian, artist, craftsperson, experimental psychologist, navigator, hunter, interior designer, explorer, guide, inventor, mechanic, airplane

pilot, anatomist, painter, graphic design artist, air traffic controller, photographer, illustrator, scout, explorer, builder.

Bodily/Kinesthetic:
Inventor, instrumentalist, dancer, juggler, actor, personal fitness trainer, typist, acrobat, athlete, programmer, mechanic, craftsperson, engineer, clown, artisan, surgeon, carpenter, forest ranger.

Musical:
Composer, performer, instrumentalist, aficionados, singer, disc jockey, conductor, band member, opera director, choir member, those who enjoy, understand or appreciate music, rock group member, dance band, music teacher, vocalist, music therapist.

Naturalist:
Geologist, Chef, landscape architect, ecotourism, birder, botanist, astronomer, anthropologist, hunter, cataloguer, guide, anatomist, farmer, gardener, animal handler, meteorologist, naturalist, biologist, wildlife illustrator.

Life Coaching Activities & Powerful Questions

Note Your Top Three Intelligences

1. _____

2. _____

3. _____

Career Map

Now make a list of all the occupations related to each of your top intelligences.

What connections can you make?

What areas have a natural connection?

Next list businesses you could create from this list.

Perception

"The man who views the world at 50 the same as he did at 20 has wasted 30 years of his life."
                                        Muhammad Ali

Perception

"What is a weed? A plant whose virtues have never been discovered."   **Unknown**

According to the Oxford Dictionary, *"perception is the act of perceiving."*

How we perceive objects, events or people depends largely on our experiences. Our experiences create our reality. Our frame of reference is defined by our experiences. If you have never read a description, seen a picture or a live Tasmanian Devil, how would you recognize one if it was in front of you?

In education when we talk about the development of the very young child we often make reference to the need for stimulation or exposure to all kinds of objects and experiences. We need these continued new experiences throughout our life in order to develop a broader perspective. As adults we too need to continually create new experiences for our self, leading to broader perspectives and opening more opportunities.

The world is constantly changing and how we see the world should also be changing. Our perceptions can sometimes keep us from moving forward, so they need to be understood, challenged and changed, if necessary.
How we perceive the people in our life and at work can influence our success in those areas. Depending on our Mind Set, our perception may be shaded with judgments and values based on a person's appearance, religion, sexual preference, socio economic status, thus, setting up barriers before we even get to know the real person.
Your clients will come to you with varying degrees of life and work perceptions, and as a life coach it is essential to help them develop an understanding of their perceptions and assist them in making shifts or change in perceptions, if needed.

Activity   Understanding and Shifting Perception

Much of this area is dependent on a combination of the other areas of the life coaching process. Helping clients make a change or shift in thinking and perception may be slow but it is necessary for change and learning to happen.

1. Clients need to become very self aware.

2. Suggest that clients expose themselves to new experiences.

3. Listen to a different radio station, new type of music.

4. Eat in a different restaurant

5. Take up a new sport, even for a brief period.

6. Try having more fun. Laugh for 5 minutes every morning.

7. Change an old habit to a new habit and practice for a month.

8. Start a fitness program.

9. Take a risk. Try it.

10. Confront your perceptions about others.

Coaching Questions Perception

1. What change do you need to make in how you see the world?

2. Are you always honest with yourself?

3. Is there anything at work or in life that you are denying?

4. How do you see the people you work with? How do they see you?

5. Are you open to change?

6. What do you need to do to be open?

7. What does being open look like?

8. If you make this change in thinking what difference will it make in your life and work?

9. What might this shift in thinking mean, in 5 years, 10 years?

10. If you were to write your eulogy what would it say?

Work/ Life Balance

"He who is everywhere, is nowhere."

Seneca

Work/ Life Balance

What do we really mean when we talk about Work/Life balance?

Work/Life balance is just as the word indicates; equal amount of time given to each area, be it work or other activities in our life.

Creating a Work/Life balance is certainly a desired state for most people but many times it may appear the ideal and unachievable. It is however essential if we are to be productive workers and get the most from our Life.

Work/Life Balance Activities

1. Keep a daily dairy. Note the number of hours you spend at work and work related activities. Also note the number of hours that you spend with family, recreational activities, and activity outside of work. Do this for two weeks. At the end of the two week period, compare the number of hours in each area work and life. If your numbers are equal or close to equal, congratulations, you have a balanced work/life. If however there is a disproportionate amount in one area, sorry, there is an imbalance and can cause you to fall and lose control.

2. Revisit your Wheel of Life. What areas can you work on to adjust your balance?

3. Don't Juggle…Select and Connect

Take these areas Selected in # 2 and focus your attention, Connect fully at work, at home and play.

Questions to Direct Life Work Balance

1. What do you want in life this week, this month?

2. What do you have to do to make this happen?

3. What are your responsibilities in life and work?

4. Are you true to these responsibilities?

5. What else can you do to create the balance?

6. Are there adjustments you can make in your actions, attitude?

7. Are you being honest with yourself?

8. What can you do today to feel better about your work?

9. What will the balanced life/ work look like?

10. Are you kind to yourself? Do you reward yourself when you accomplish tasks?

11. Where can you delegate?

12. What can you delete?

13. What is a normal work week?

14. Why do you want life/work balance?

13. Life is good, could it be better?

Focus and Attention

"Energy flows where attention goes."
Law of Attraction

Focus and Attending

We cannot succeed in life or work without Focus and Attention.

How important are these two concepts to career and life achievement?

What part do they play in our life and work?

As an employee do you give your work full Focus and Attention?

As a manager, business owner, do you know if your employees are fully Focused and Attending?

If we are to achieve what we want to achieve we need to Focus and Attend.

What is Focus?

If you have ever looked through a camera lens or binoculars you know you have to adjust the focus to see clearly. And for the most part, one object or subject is the Focus of your Attention, be it out in nature or at a sports event or concert.

What is Attending?

Back in the mid 90's I leased a black Mazda 626. It looked so unique in the parking lot. I didn't remember seeing this car before. However, shortly after leaving the car dealership I saw a black 626 and then I saw another, and everywhere I looked I saw a black 626. They were there all the time but I hadn't attended to them, they were not in my focus.

I come from a teaching background and how often did I and my colleagues say to our students, "pay attention". What were we asking them to do? Did they really know what that was and how to attend? Were they attending in their own way?

If you listen to the color commentators in sport, I will use golf as it is a favorite of mine, you will hear them comment on how focused an individual player is. Golf, I think is a good example because it is an individual sport within the context of other players, paralleling life to a degree.

Focusing on what is happening at the immediate time is an essential part of the game. Some may call it concentration but it is Focus and Attending. And just as in sport, to succeed in life we have to develop the skills of Focusing and Attending.

How well do you focus at work?

What do you attend to at work?

What should you attend to at work?

Do you set aside time to focus and attend to tasks?

Do tasks go unfinished due to lack of Focus and Attention?

Activities for Focusing and Attending

1. On your way to work decide to focus on one thing. Pick a color, a model of car. Count just how many times you see the object of your Attention.

2. Go for your usual walk, this time listen for sounds around you. Make a mental note. Write out the list later. Next time you walk attend a little more, how many more sounds did you here? Note them.

3. If you have children, focus on them and attend to every word they say. This activity will not only help you develop your skills of attending and focusing, it will bring you closer to your child.

4. At work adjust your focus and attend to what you have to do, you will find work being completed in a more effective timely manner.

5. Focus on yourself. Attend to how you attend and focus. How good are you?

Affirmations

"Our thoughts form our actions."

Coach Phyllis

Affirmations

Choose an affirmation that resonates with you, write on a sticky or memorize and repeat several times throughout your day. Affirmations help us stay positive, change our language and help change our beliefs and way of behaving. They help set these positive thoughts about ourselves in our sub-conscience, leading us to achieve our goals. They are always stated in the present tense.

1. Revisit your vision, what do you want to become. Name it and place it in this affirmation.
 I am the very best (name) in my city, prov/state, country.

2. *This is the best day of my life.*

3. *I am happy, healthy and wise.*

4. *I am full of power and potential.*

5. *I am surrounded by caring, loving people.*

6. *I can do it.*

7. *I feel great about myself.*

8. *I am a loving and kind person.*

9. *I am unique and special.*

10. *I deserve the best of life.*

11. *I make my own choices in life.*

12. *I am the best I can be.*

Write your own daily affirmations for your life.

1._____
_____
_____
_____
_____
_____

2._____
_____
_____
_____
_____
_____

3._____
_____
_____
_____
_____
_____

Post them where you can see them. Repeat often!

It must be noted that as powerful as Affirmations are they need Action.

Inspirational Quotes

Or

Food For Thought

*Quotes can be used in many ways.
Here are some of my favorite quotes and ways I use them.*

1. *I use these quotes in my coaching sessions.*

2. *I use them for my own self reflection.*

3. *I use them as the basis of an article.*

4. *I use them as a thread in writing a Blog.*

5. *I use them as a Twitter.*

6. *I copy and distribute at workshops.*

7. *I use them personally as daily reminders by placing them on my office wall.*

8. *I use them in emails to clients.*

Think of ways you might use these quotes. I think of them as food for thought.

Try one a day!

Inspirational Quotes

We can do anything we want to do if we stick to it long enough.
                                    Helen Keller

If people only knew how hard I worked, they wouldn't be so amazed.
                                    Michaelangelo

The beginning is half of every action.
                                    Greek proverb

It sometimes seems that intense desire creates not only its own opportunities, but its own talent.
                                    Eric Hoffer

Our aspirations are our possibilities.
                                    Robert Browning

Always bear in mind that your own resolution to succeed is more important than any other thing.
                                    Abraham Lincoln

Most people know what they want but they don't know how to achieve it.
                                              Coach Phyllis

If you think you can or you can't, you are right.
                          Henry Ford

*There are high spots in all of our lives
and most of them have come about through
encouragement from someone else.
I don't care how great, how famous or
successful a man or woman may be,
each hungers for applause.*

George M. Adams

I have no special talents, I am only passionately curious.

Albert Einstein

People are not motivated by failure; they are motivated by achievement and recognition.

F. Fournies

Everyone has an invisible sign hanging from their neck saying: Make me feel important.

Mary Kay Ash

I can live for two months on one good compliment.

                                                  Mark Twain

Life is not easy. It can seem very much like a balancing act, so why not develop the Balancing Skills to walk that tight rope?

                                                  Coach Phyllis

Life is either a daring adventure or nothing.

                                                  Helen Keller

Chance favors the prepared mind.

                                                  Louis Pasteur

Do or do not, there is no try.

                                                  Yoda, Star Wars

Don't cry because it's over,
Smile because it happened.

                                                  Dr. Seuss

Failure is not an option.

                                                  NASA

Inspiration exists, but it has to find us working.

                                                  Picasso

If you're going through hell, keep going.

> **Sir Winston Churchill**

To be able to look back on one's life in satisfaction is to live twice.

> **Khalil Gibran**

Everyman dies. Not everyman really lives.

> **William Ross Waller**

We live but a fraction of our life.

> **Henry David Thoreau**

I've learned that making a living is not the same as making a " life."

> **Maya Angelou**

Live as you would have wished to live when you are dying.

> **Unknown**

Live your life and forget your age.

> **Norman Peale**

They may forget what you said but they will never forget how you made them feel.

> **Carl W. Buechner**

Goal Work Sheets (cont)

Goals Continued

Goal Two Action Steps

Action Step One
_____
_____
_____

Action Step Two
_____
_____
_____

Action Step Three
_____
_____

Action Step Four
_____
_____
_____

Action Step Five
_____
_____
_____

Goal Three Action Steps

Action Step One
_____
_____
_____

Action Step Two
_____
_____
_____

Action Step Three
_____
_____
_____

Action Step Four
_____
_____
_____

Action Step Five
_____
_____

Goal Four Action Steps

Action Step One
_____
_____
_____

Action Step Two
_____
_____
_____

Action Step Three
_____
_____

Action Step Four
_____

Action Step Five

_____
_____
_____

Goals Continued

Goal Five Action Steps

Action Step One

_____
_____
_____

Action Step Two

_____
_____
_____

Action Step Three

_____
_____

Action Step Four

_____
_____

Action Step Five

_____
_____
_____

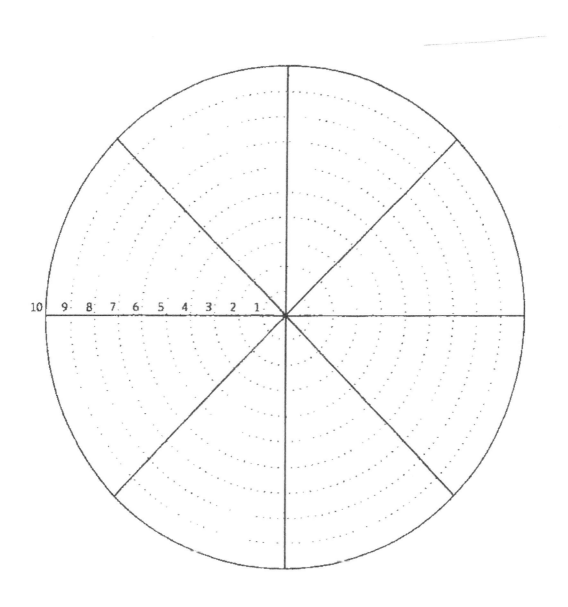

Wheel of Life

What's Next in My Life?

What's Next?

What I have learned about Me
_____
_____
_____
_____
_____
_____
_____
_____
_____

What I have learned about Me and My Family (Work)
_____
_____
_____
_____
_____
_____
_____
_____

What I have learned about Me and Work
_____
_____
_____
_____
_____
_____
_____

Where is new Learning needed?

_____
_____
_____
_____
_____

Next Steps?

_____
_____
_____
_____
_____

What do I see for myself next year?

_____
_____
_____
_____
_____

What is my life like in 5 years?

_____
_____
_____
_____
_____

What Next for Me?

_____
_____
_____
_____
_____
_____
_____
_____

1. Write your thoughts in point form daily.

2. Keep on track.

3. Stick with it, Persist

4. Only you can create your Future.

5. Go for it!

Conclusion

My hope is that you will use my *Life Coaching Skills* and continue to develop and enhance them. Like any skill they need to be continually practiced to be perfected. If you use them regularly for a month they should become a part of your everyday life.

Please share them with family and friends.

You will find that as you read my book, *Life Coaching Activities and Powerful Questions,* you will have thoughts or ideas about your own life and life in general. I invite you to note these. This is new learning and will contribute to more personal growth.

Life is a Challenge. Are you ready?

Life Coaching Articles
By Phyllis Reardon, M.Ed.
Life Coach

I am including a selection of my Life Coaching Articles.

Feel free to share with your clients but please reference me as the author.

Coach Phyllis

Achieving Success Through Life Coaching

By Phyllis Reardon M.E.d. Life Coach

"Most people know exactly what they want but they don't know how to achieve it."
                         Coach Phyllis

Success can be defined in many ways depending on the focus and standards of the individual.

Webster defines success as: 'The achievement of something desired, intended, or attempted.'

To professional golfer success might be winning another Masters tournament, to a novice golfer it might be breaking 100. To a professional musician success might be performing on Broadway or the West End, to a beginning musician it may be a good practice session. To the seasoned business person success might be a million dollar contract; to a beginning entrepreneur it might be that first client.

Success meets us where we are and takes us further by motivating and pushing us in the direction we so desire. What is the old adage….success breeds success.

For most people success comes when they accomplish what they set out to achieve. Easier said than done?

Success needs a desire to change but it also needs the right tools.

The key to success is having a clear plan of direction and being ready to adjust along the way. Did you know that the space shuttle is off course 90% of the time? Navigational adjustments are continuous. We, too, have to be ready for these adjustments.

Success begins with good goal setting. Goals however will only be achieved with appropriate strategies and implementation plans suitable to both the goals and the goal setter. Most New Year resolutions fail not due to lack of desire on part of the individuals who set them, they want these changes to happen; no they fail because proper strategies were not put in place.

Implementation strategies and processes are as important as the goals themselves, as they create movement in the right direction. This movement toward the goal creates motivation which in turn creates more movement toward the desired goal. Another major part of these strategies is accountability or monitoring, whether that be self monitoring or by a life coach. Accountability keeps actions on track and moving forward.

Successes will happen but only if proper goals and strategies are put in place!

Let me help you achieve your goals.

Contact me, Coach Phyllis   phyllis@coachphyllis.com

Phyllis Reardon, Life Coach
CoachPhyllis.com Inc. © 2009
www.coachphyllis.com

How Do You Measure Your Life in a Year?

Phyllis Reardon M.Ed.
Life Coach

Can we really manage time or do we have to learn to manage our self?

I want you to think about this for a moment or a minute or even an hour, whatever your time permits. Can you possibly manage time? What does the word manage mean? Can you make the day longer? Can you make a work day shorter? Can you delay your 30th, 40th, 50th birthday? Time and tide wait for no man or woman.

Think about the concept of time. How long has the earth been here? How long ago was the first member of your family born? When did your family come to this new world? How old is your city? How long did it take to get your education? How many minutes does it take to cook your favorite meal? How minutes does it take to walk to the corner store?

Time, time, time. Jim Croce sings "If I could save time in a bottle" If only, if only. We need to remember in our self management that there is only one IF in L'IF'E and that is embedded in the middle of the word.

The fact is that there are 24 hours in a day or 1,440 minutes with 168 hours in a week. If you have seen the musical Rent you will know from the song, *Seasons of Love* that there are five hundred twenty-five thousand six hundred minutes in a year. How do you measure your life in a year?

So just how do you get everything done that you hope to do? Well first you have to move beyond hope and go directly to planning and not just wishy - washy planning but good hard direct Strategic Planning. This planning must incorporate self management.

Are you getting the most from all your minutes? In this cell phone/iphone culture we are very keen to get the most of every minute. How do we do this in life?

1. Create a daily To-Do-List

2. Place in a highly visible space

3. Review each day

4. Scratch off when completed

5. Review, Revamp, Rewrite weekly

Check your minutes!!!

If you are interested in finding out how to better self manage or get the most from your minutes, please contact me.

Contact: Phyllis Reardon, BA.(Ed.); M.Ed.
      www.coachphyllis.com Inc Copyright 2008
              Life Coach
            phyllis@coachphyllis.com
             www.coachphyllis.com

Life Coaching Questions For Reaching your Full Potential

Phyllis Reardon B.A., M.Ed.
Life Coach

Questions direct our life and are an extremely important part of the Life Coaching process. Questioning directs and challenges clients to become more aware of their potential and to help them create ways to achieve life/work success.

I invite you to use these questions in your life and share them with others.

1. What do you really, really, really want?

2. Why do you want it?

3. What is success to you?

4. What does it look like?

5. How will you know when you have become successful?

6. How will you know when you have found it?

7. What is holding you back from getting it?

8. Do you believe you can get it?

9. What motivates you?

10. What are your intelligences and talents?

11. How can you make the greatest difference in your own life?

12. Who do you have to Become in order to achieve what you Want to achieve?

13. What has to be modified within you?

14. What change in your thinking has to take place?

15. What change in your personality has to take place?

16. What new knowledge do you need to gain?

17. What new skills do you need to learn?

If you would like to find out more about Life Coaching please contact me.

Contact: Phyllis Reardon, BA.(Ed.); M.Ed.
     www.coachphyllis.com Inc Copyright 2008
               Life Coach
               phyllis@coachphyllis.com
   www.coachphyllis.com

The Author

Phyllis E. Reardon is a life coach who has spent all of her working life in the enhancement of others' lives. Through her many years as a parent, teacher, counselor and life coach she has come to understand that many individuals have much more potential than they believe they have. Increasing this potential is a passion for Phyllis.

Phyllis lives in Newfoundland and Labrador, Canada and can be easily reached at her email, phyllis@coachphyllis.com

www.coachphyllis.com

Made in the USA
Las Vegas, NV
03 September 2023